Landing at Ellis Island

By Holly Karapetkova

Illustrated By Pete McDonnell

ROURKE PUBLISHING

Vero Beach, Florida 32964

www.rourkepublishing.com

PHOTO CREDITS: © fobos: Title page, pages 26, 27, 28, 29, 30, 31, 32; © Library of Congress: pages 4, 5, 26, 28; © John Carvalho: page 27

Edited by Katherine M. Thal
Illustrated by Pete McDonnell
Art Direction by Renee Brady
Page Layout by Heather Botto

Library of Congress Cataloging-in-Publication Data

Karapetkova, Holly.
 Landing at Ellis Island / Holly Karapetkova.
    p. cm. -- (Eye on history graphic illustrated)
 Includes bibliographical references and index.
 ISBN 978-1-60694-443-1 (alk. paper)
 ISBN 978-1-60694-552-0 (soft cover)
 1. Ellis Island Immigration Station (N.Y. and N.J.)--History--Juvenile literature. 2. United States--Emigration and immigration--History--Juvenile literature. I. Title.
 JV6484.K37 2010
 304.8'73--dc22

                               2009020506

Printed in the USA
CG/CG

3 4015 07030 0338

www.rourkepublishing.com - rourke@rourkepublishing.com
Post Office Box 643328 Vero Beach, Florida 32964

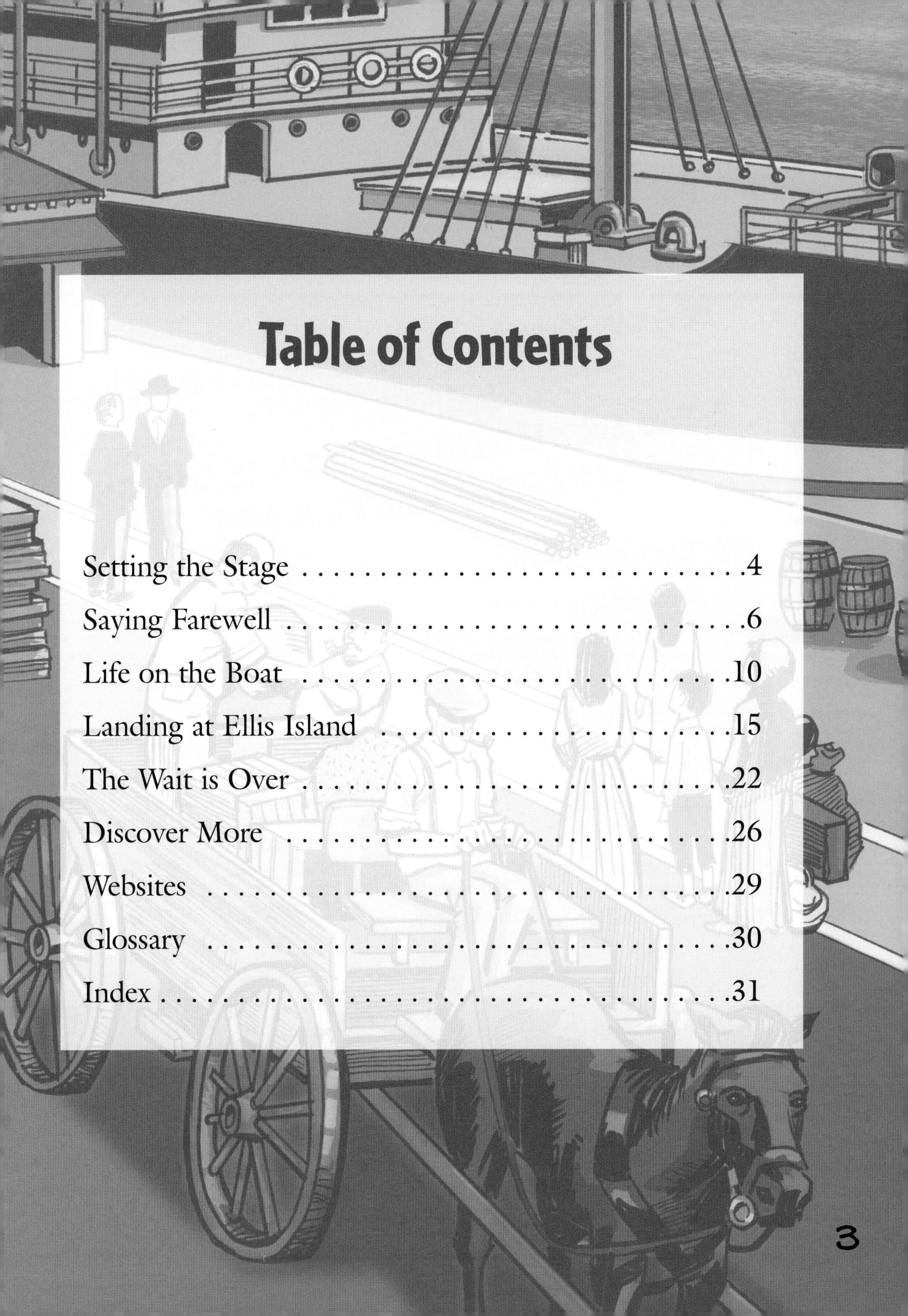

Table of Contents

New York Times Gazette

Saturday

Issue 7   Volume 11

January 2, 1892

NEW IMMIGRATION BUILDINGS OPENED YESTERDAY

New buildings for the Immigration Bureau on Ellis Island are now ready for use. Officials of that department moved in yesterday. The employees reported early, and each was shown to his place by the superintendent or his chief clerk. Colonel Weber was on the island at 8 o'clock, and went on a tour of inspection to see that the department was ready to receive its first group of immigrants.

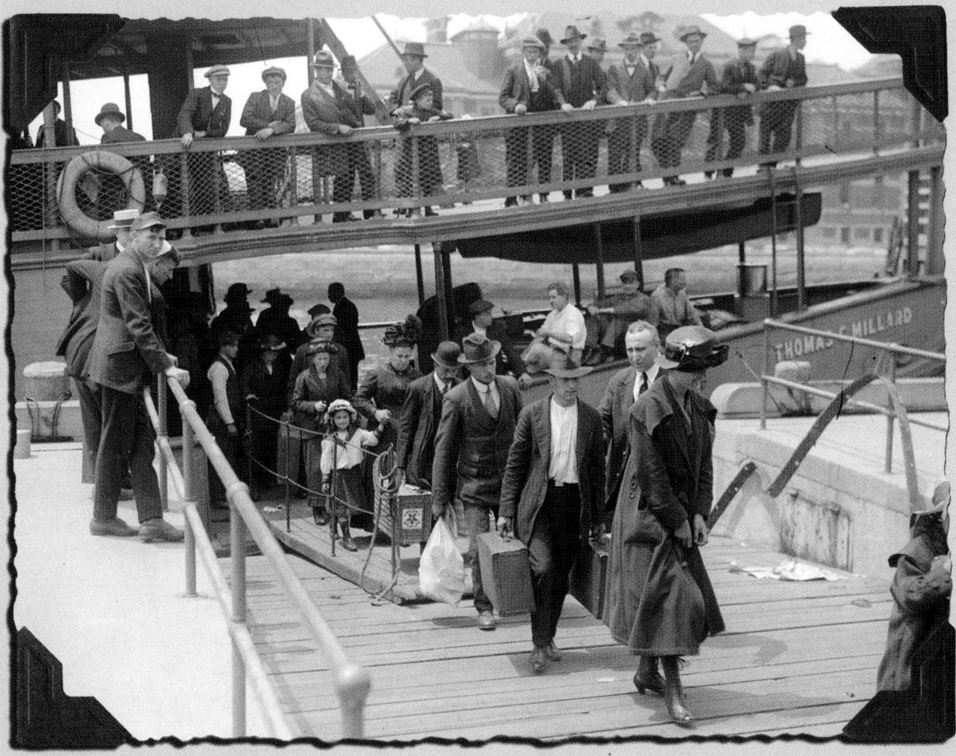
THOMAS F. MILLARD

Immigrants arrived at Ellis Island with only what they could carry.

From 1892 to 1954, Ellis Island was America's main entry station for new **immigrants**. During that time, over 12 million immigrants entered the United States through the island. Some of them came to escape political **oppression** in Europe and Asia. Some came to escape war and violence. Others, like the characters of this story, came to escape **poverty** and an unfair **class** system. They came to find work, freedom, and a better life.

The United States government built Ellis Island so that it could control who was allowed into the country. The government was afraid that criminals and people with dangerous diseases might try to enter. At Ellis Island, such immigrants were sent back to their native countries. Very few people who passed through Ellis Island were sent away, but everyone worried about the possibility. Their time on Ellis Island was mixed with dreams of a new life in America, along with the fear that those dreams might not come true. For this reason, Ellis Island became known as the *Island of Hope, Island of Tears*.

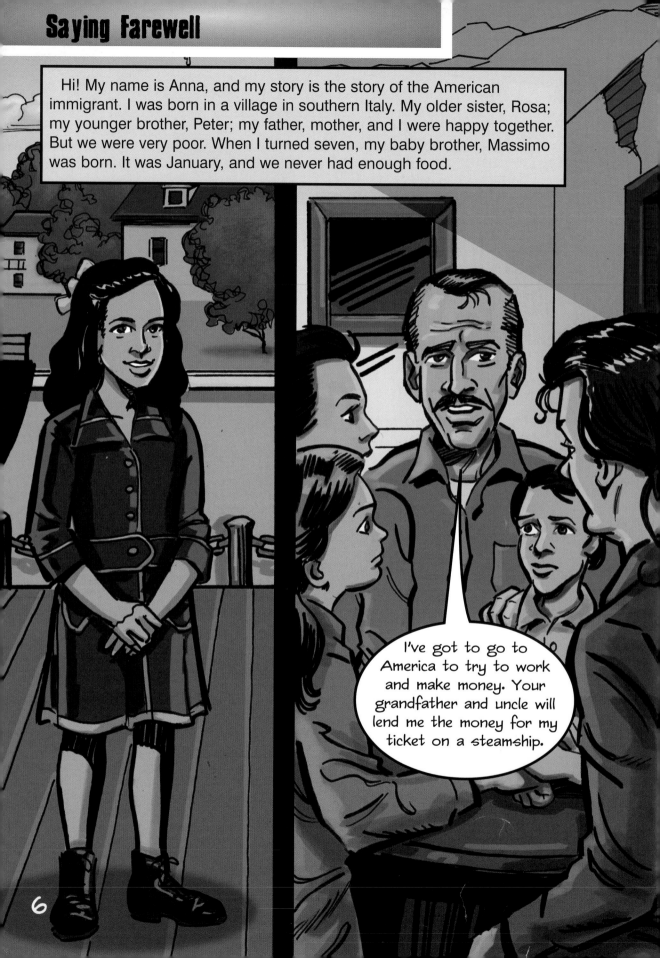

Hi! My name is Anna, and my story is the story of the American immigrant. I was born in a village in southern Italy. My older sister, Rosa; my younger brother, Peter; my father, mother, and I were happy together. But we were very poor. When I turned seven, my baby brother, Massimo was born. It was January, and we never had enough food.

I've got to go to America to try to work and make money. Your grandfather and uncle will lend me the money for my ticket on a steamship.

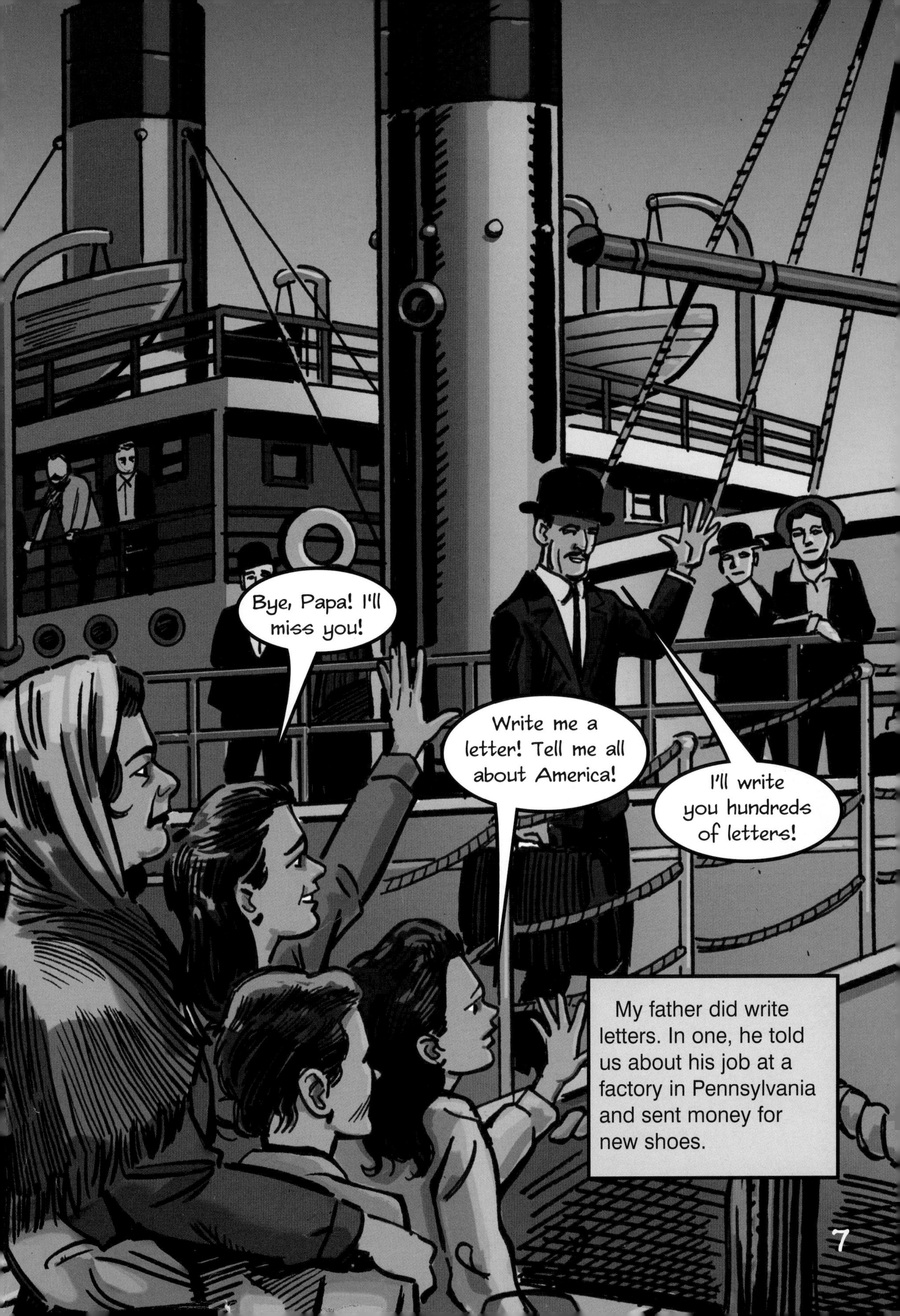
Bye, Papa! I'll miss you!
Write me a letter! Tell me all about America!
I'll write you hundreds of letters!
My father did write letters. In one, he told us about his job at a factory in Pennsylvania and sent money for new shoes.

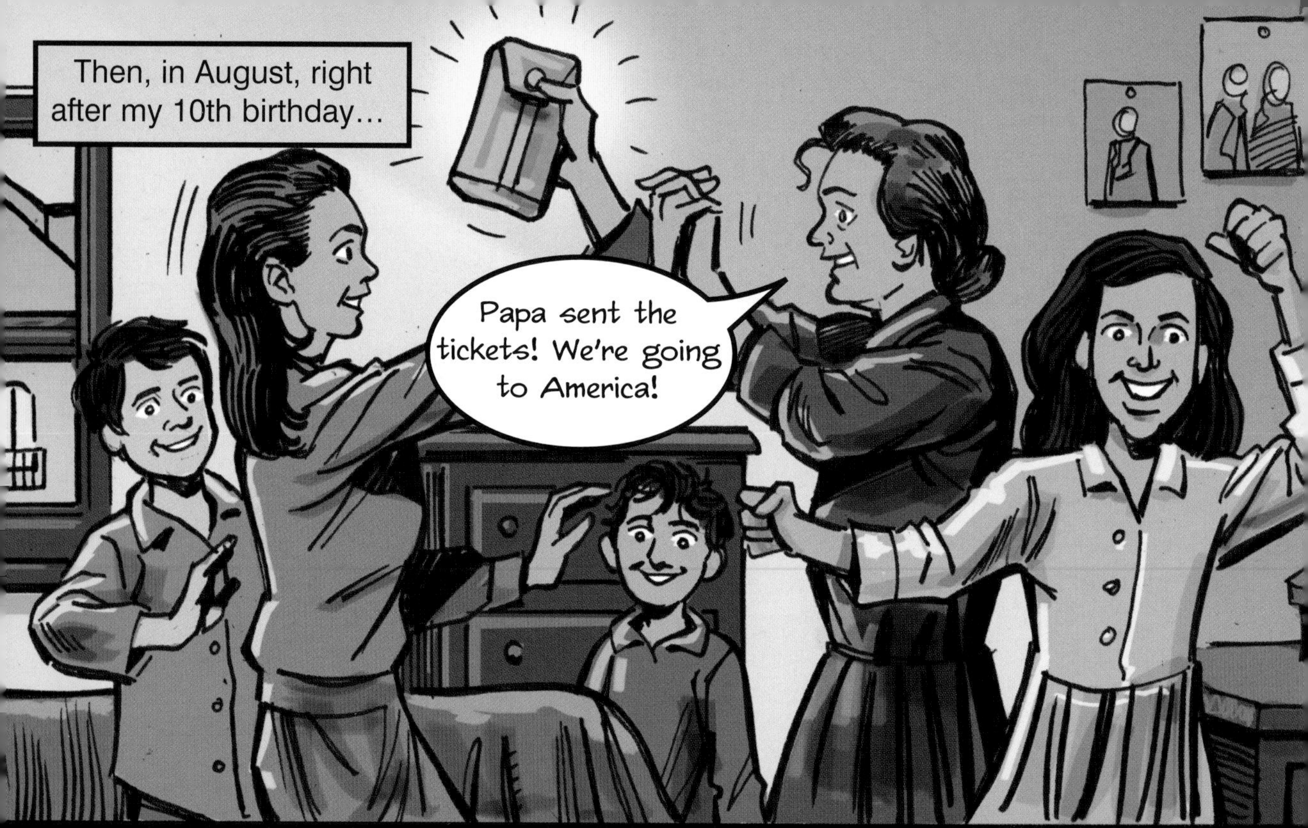
Then, in August, right after my 10th birthday…
Papa sent the tickets! We're going to America!

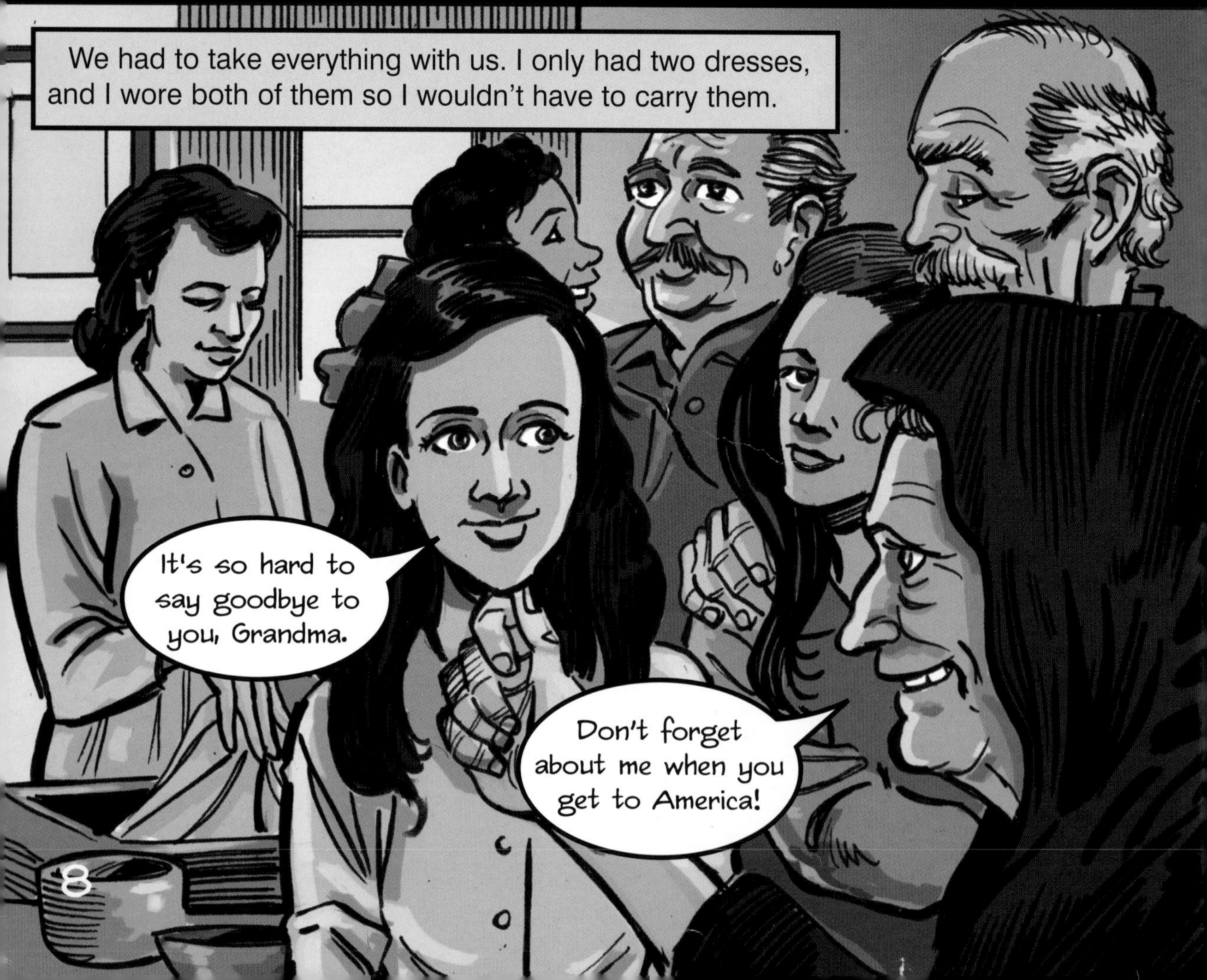
We had to take everything with us. I only had two dresses, and I wore both of them so I wouldn't have to carry them.
It's so hard to say goodbye to you, Grandma.
Don't forget about me when you get to America!

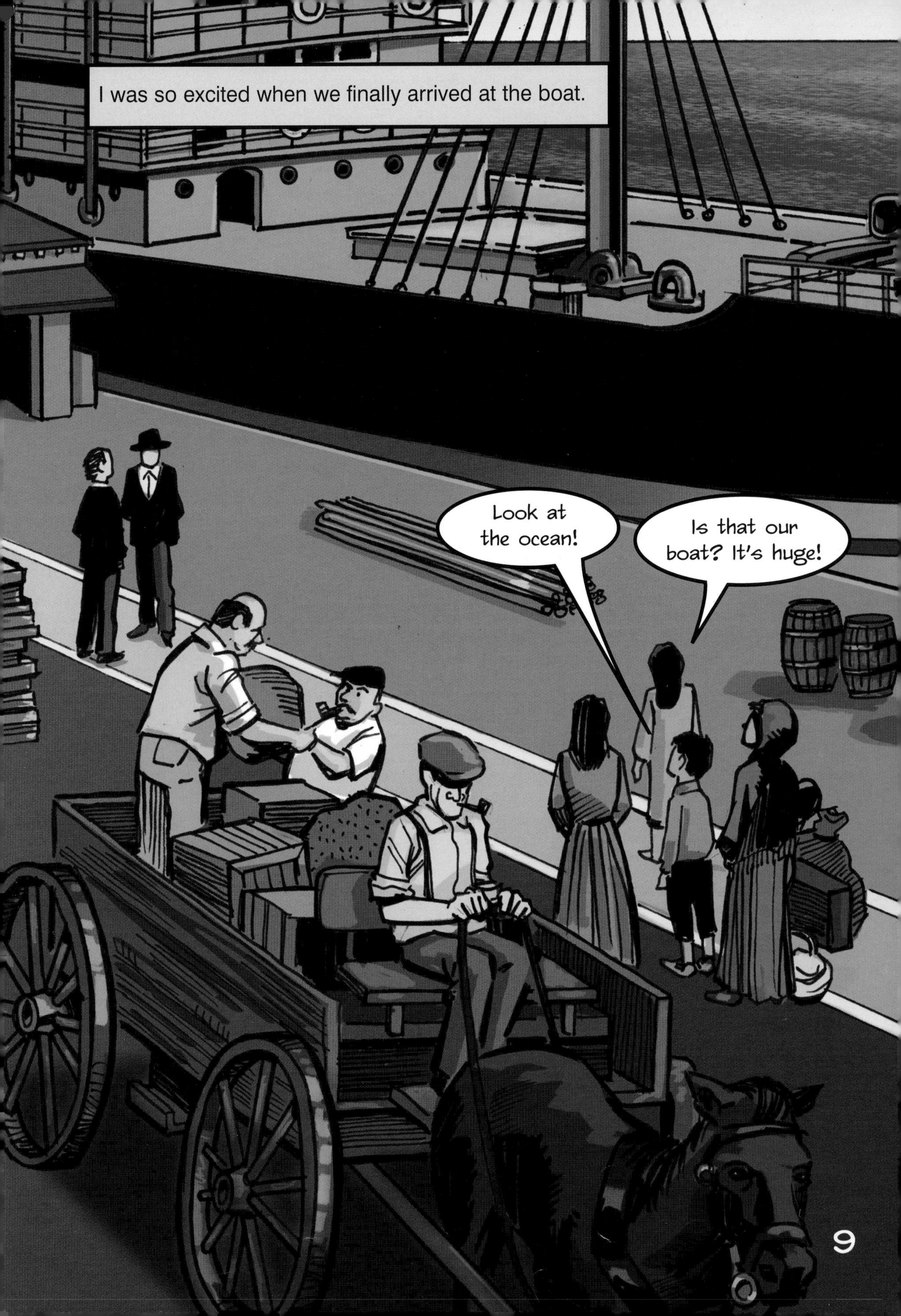
I was so excited when we finally arrived at the boat.
Look at the ocean!
Is that our boat? It's huge!

Life on the Boat

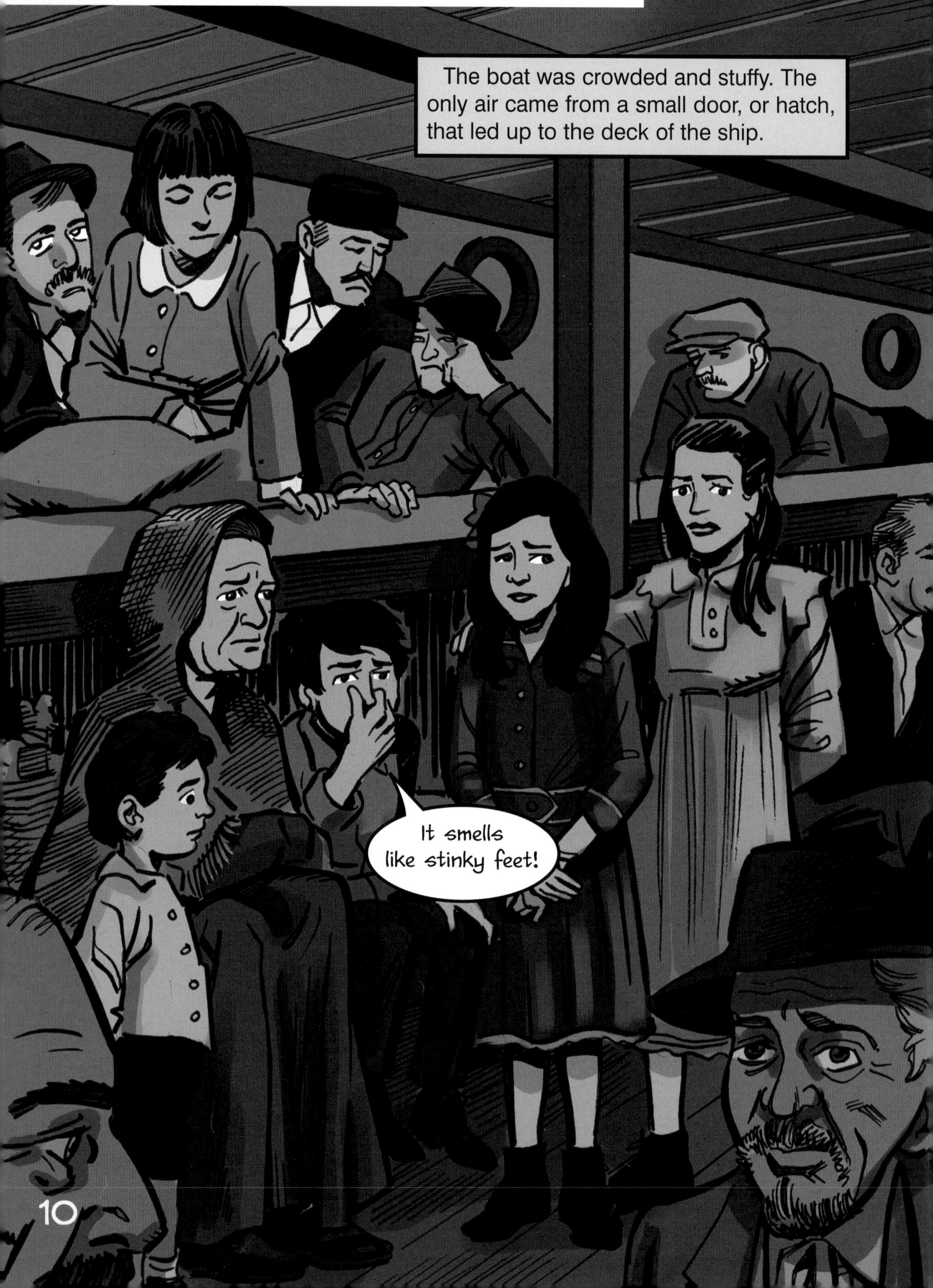
The boat was crowded and stuffy. The only air came from a small door, or hatch, that led up to the deck of the ship.
It smells like stinky feet!

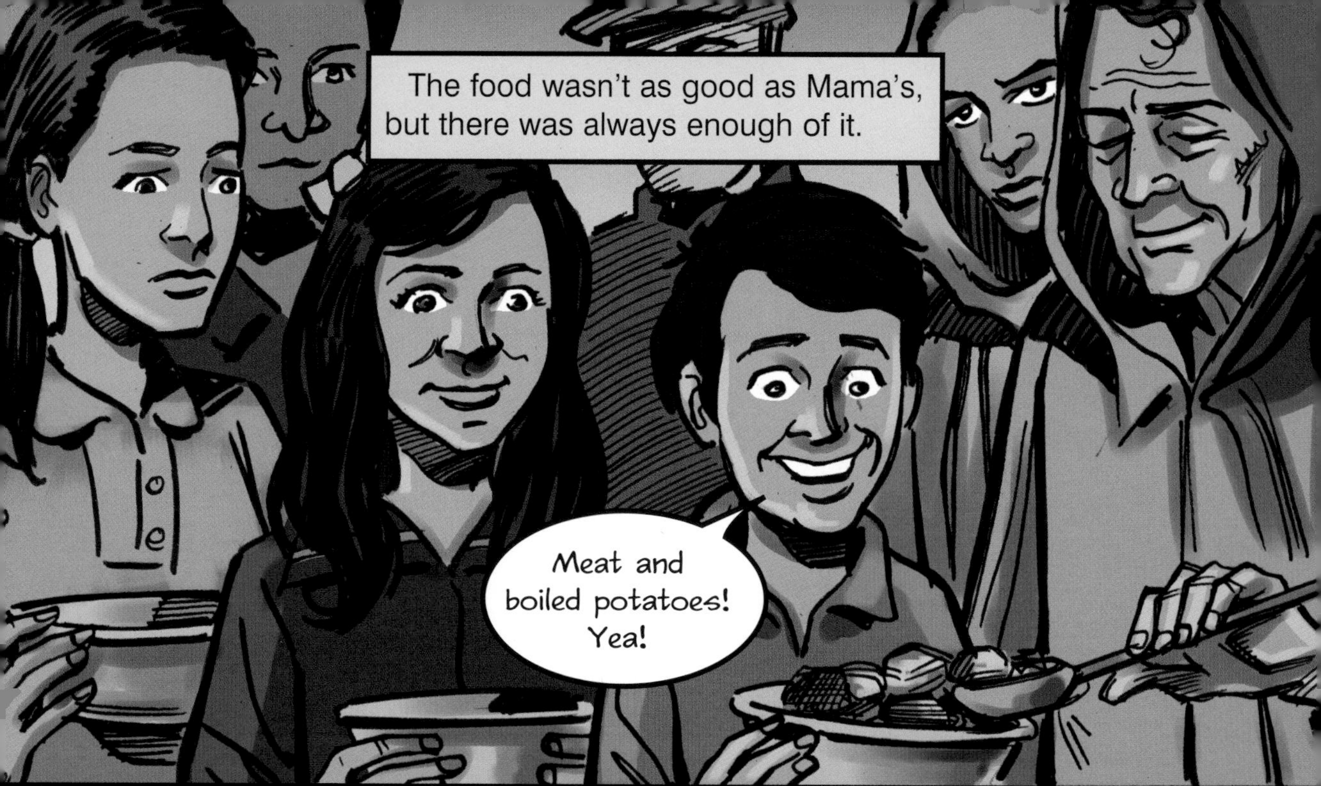
The food wasn't as good as Mama's, but there was always enough of it.
Meat and boiled potatoes! Yea!

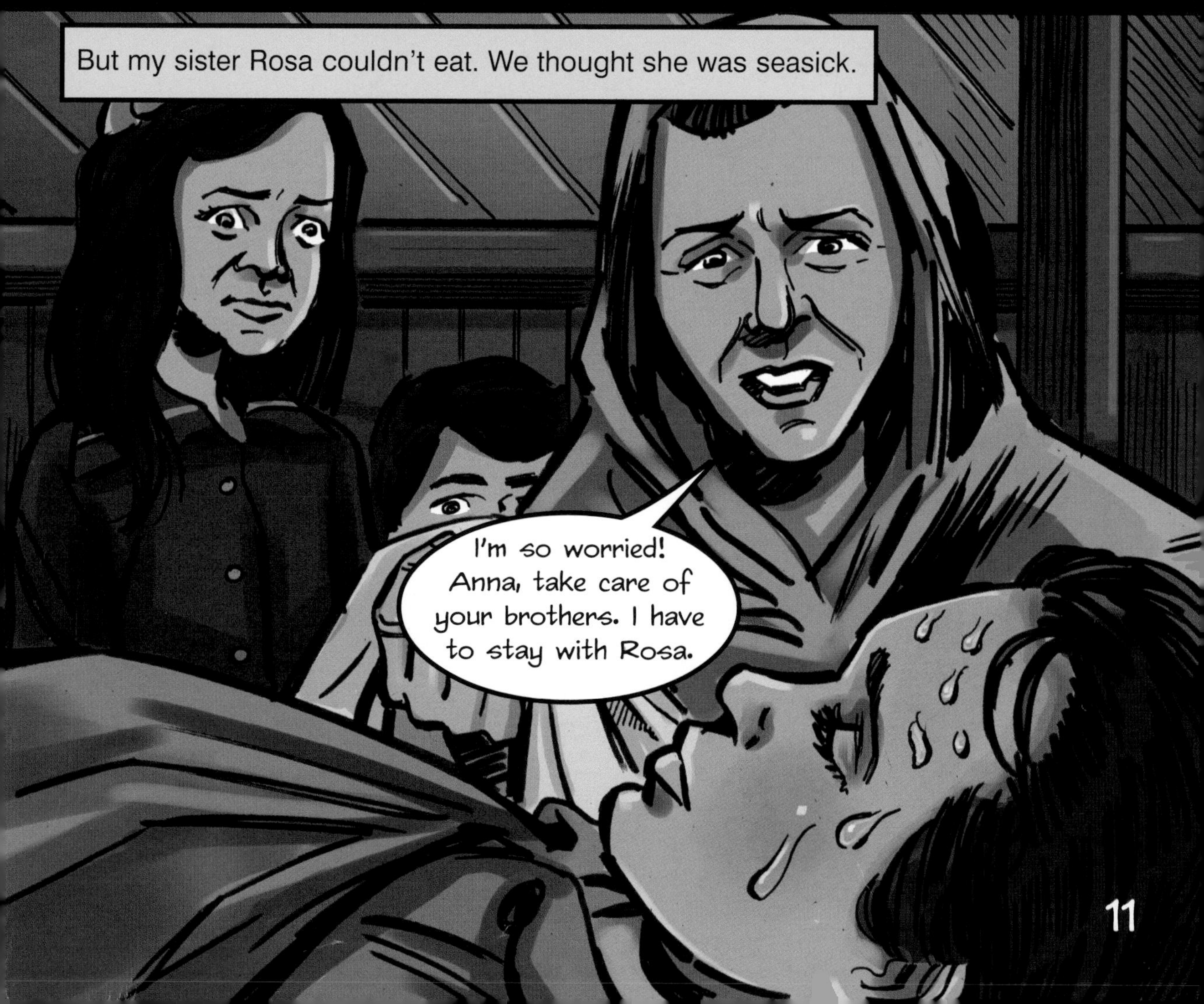
But my sister Rosa couldn't eat. We thought she was seasick.
I'm so worried! Anna, take care of your brothers. I have to stay with Rosa.

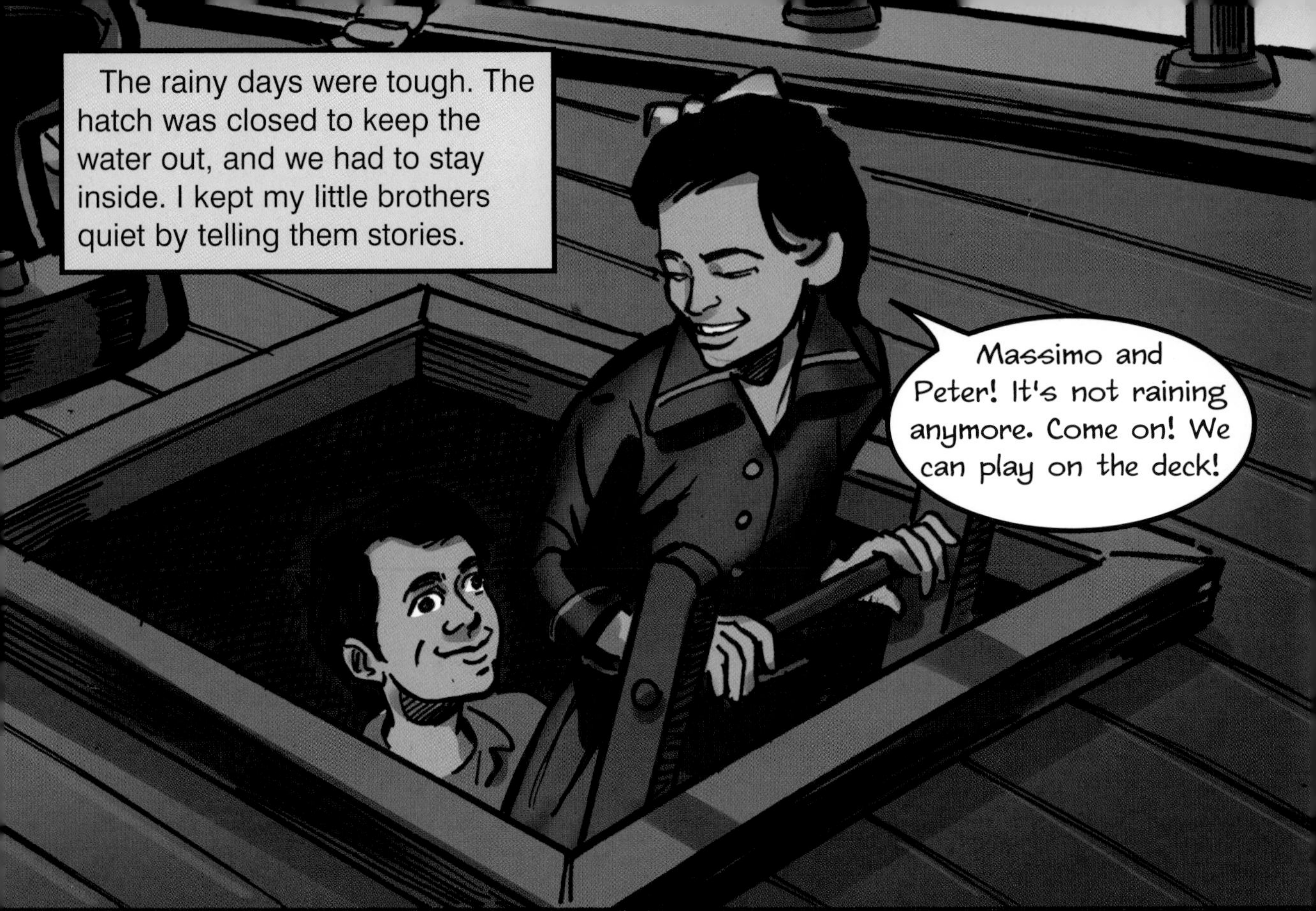
The rainy days were tough. The hatch was closed to keep the water out, and we had to stay inside. I kept my little brothers quiet by telling them stories.
Massimo and Peter! It's not raining anymore. Come on! We can play on the deck!

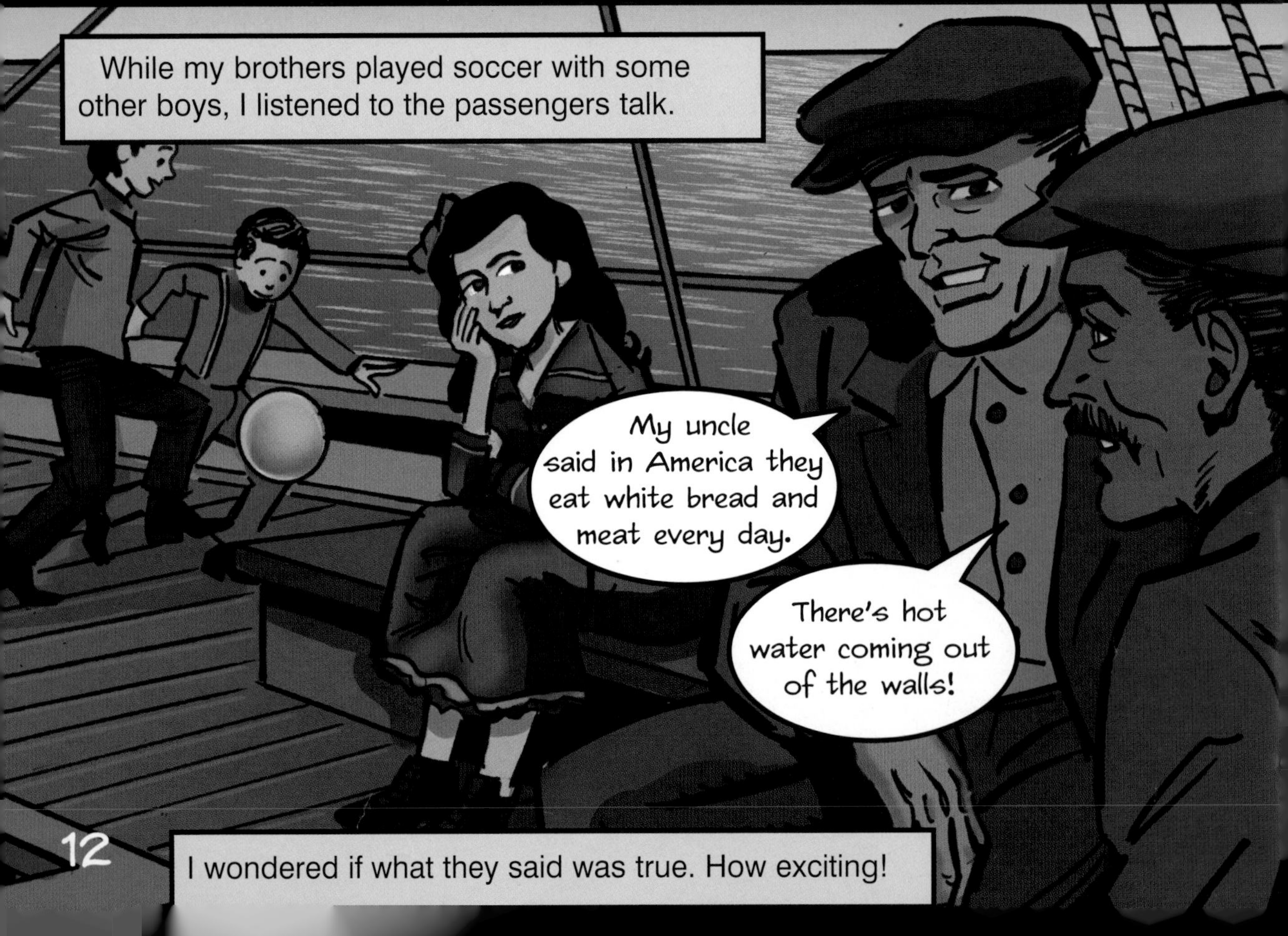
While my brothers played soccer with some other boys, I listened to the passengers talk.
My uncle said in America they eat white bread and meat every day.
There's hot water coming out of the walls!
I wondered if what they said was true. How exciting!

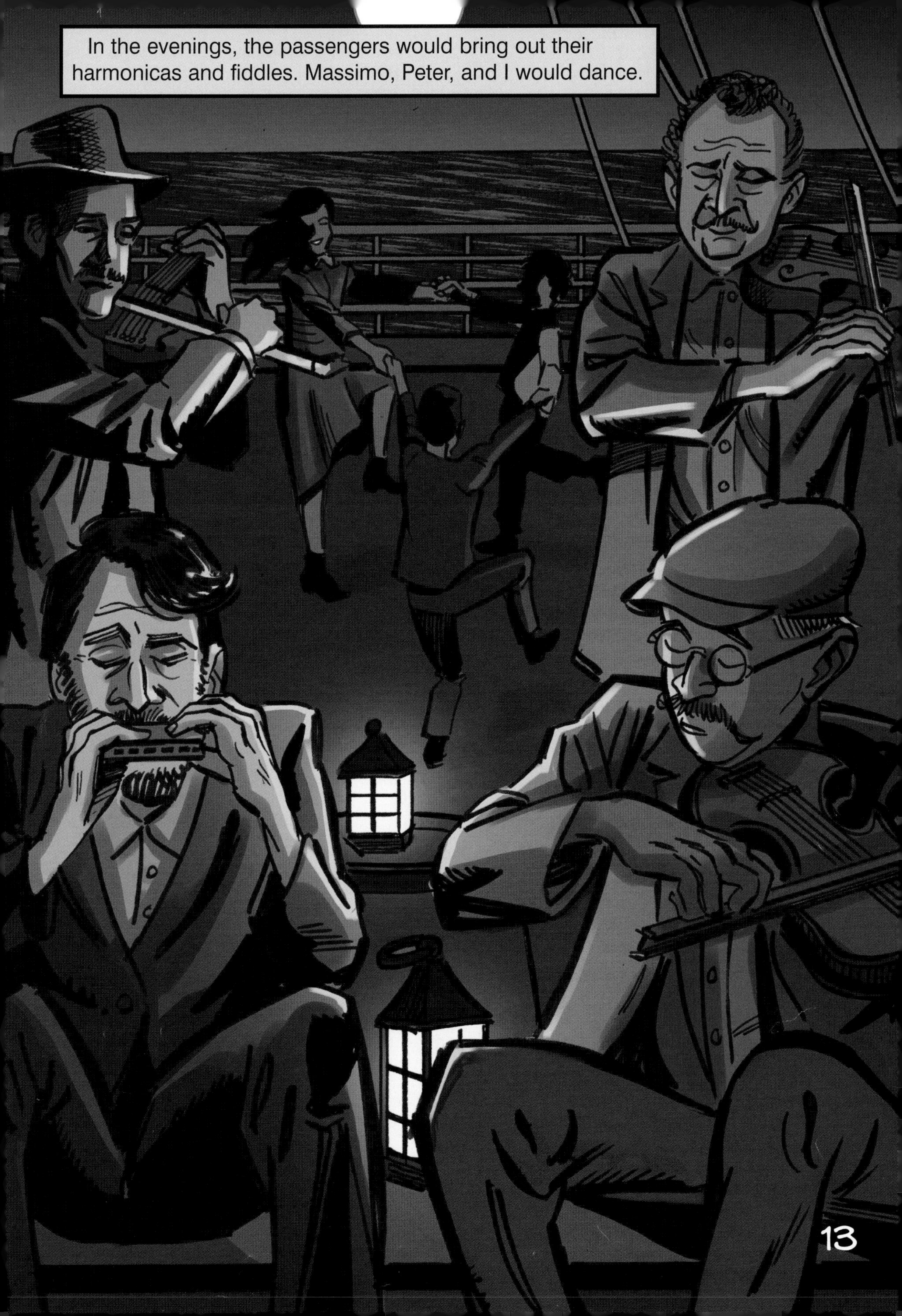
In the evenings, the passengers would bring out their harmonicas and fiddles. Massimo, Peter, and I would dance.

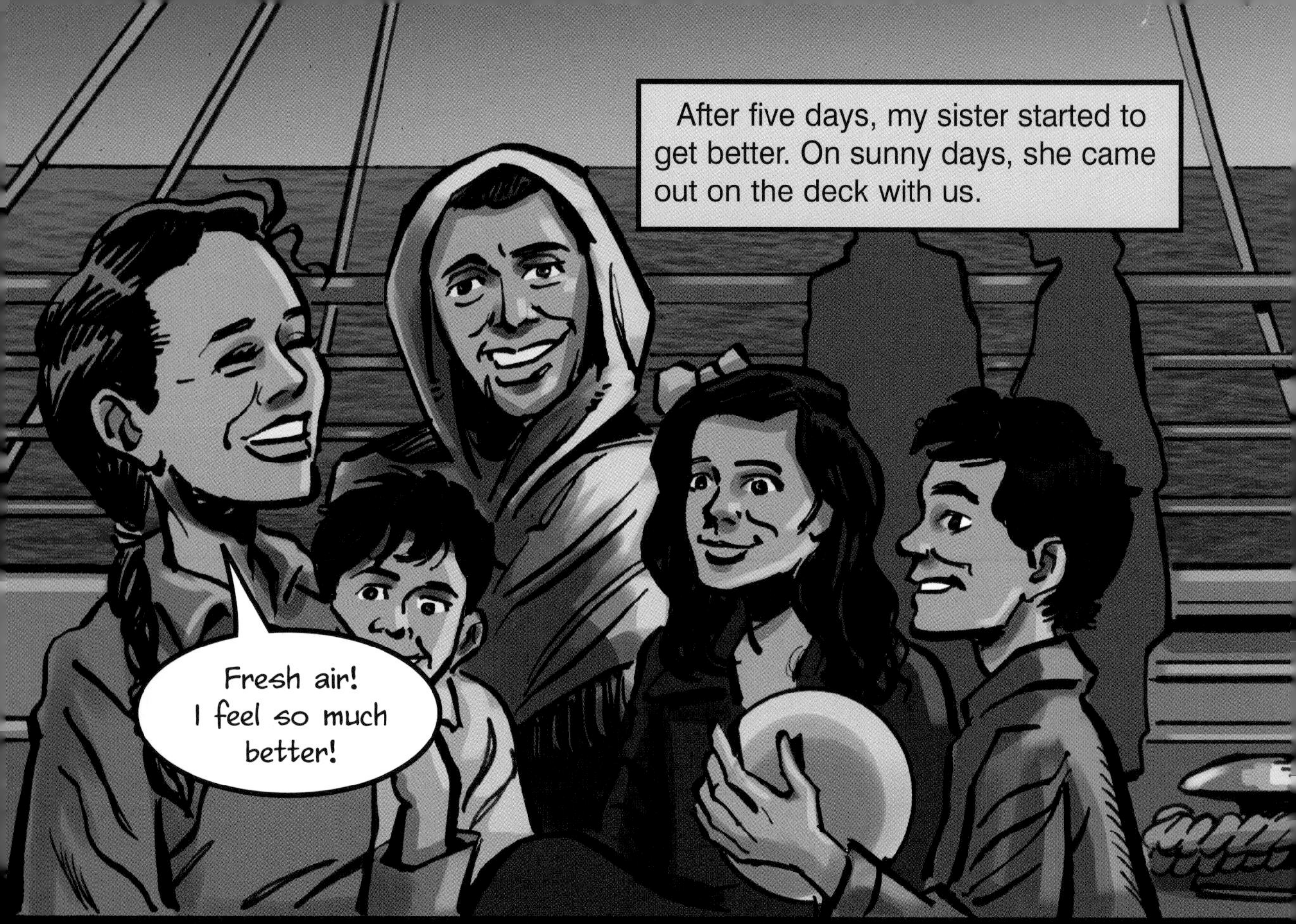
After five days, my sister started to get better. On sunny days, she came out on the deck with us.
Fresh air! I feel so much better!

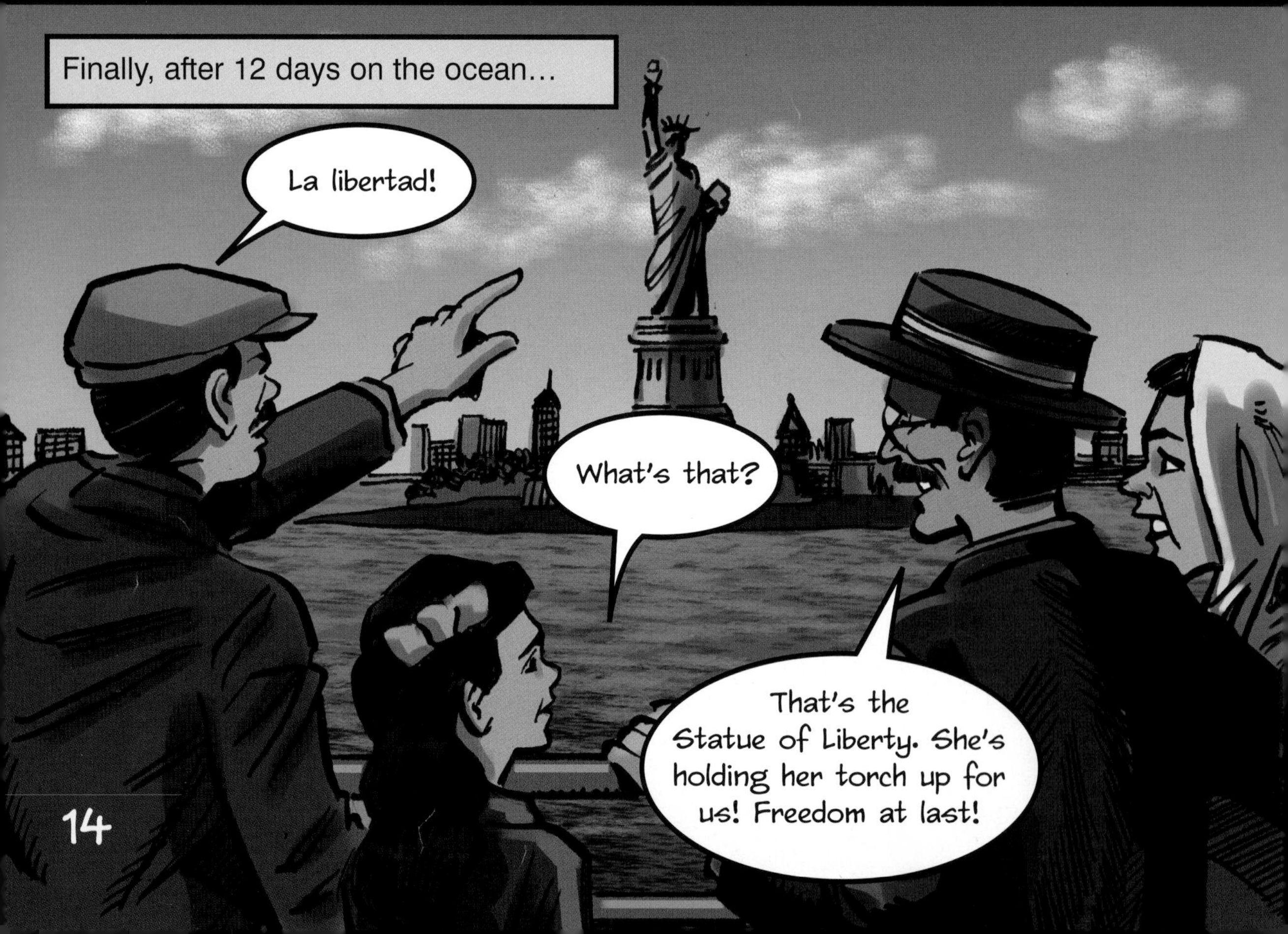
Finally, after 12 days on the ocean…
La libertad!
What's that?
That's the Statue of Liberty. She's holding her torch up for us! Freedom at last!

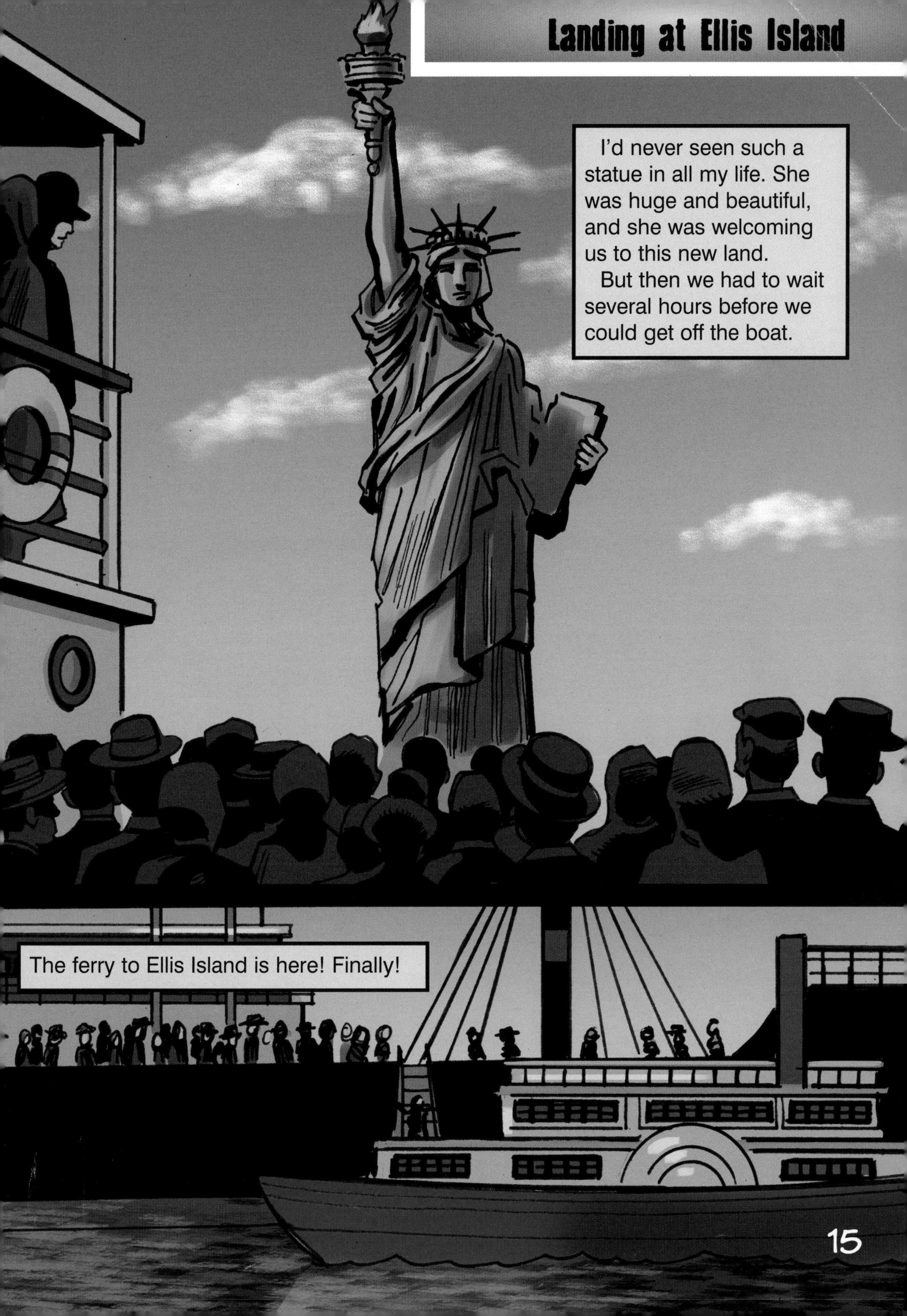
Landing at Ellis Island
I'd never seen such a statue in all my life. She was huge and beautiful, and she was welcoming us to this new land.
But then we had to wait several hours before we could get off the boat.
The ferry to Ellis Island is here! Finally!

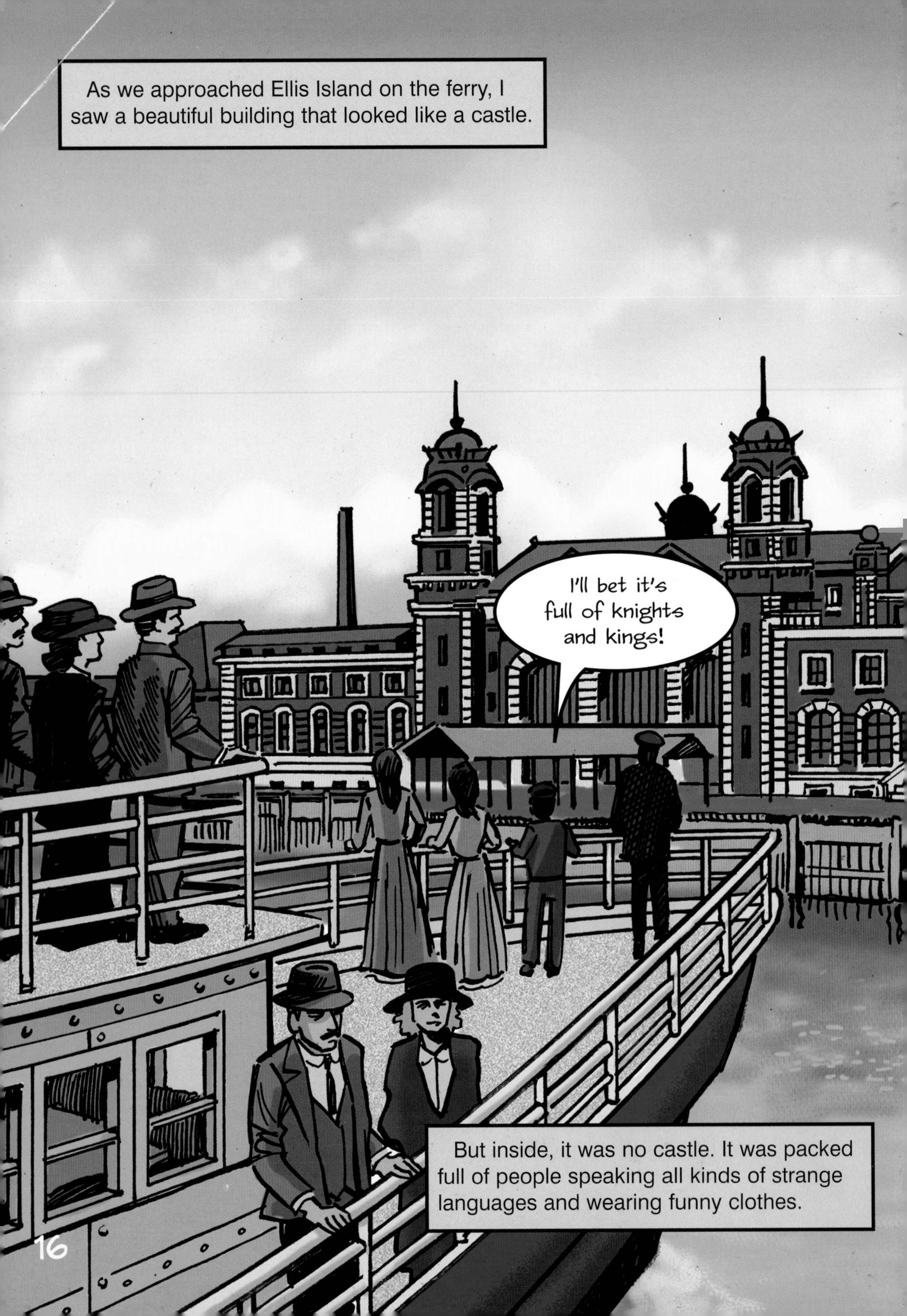
As we approached Ellis Island on the ferry, I saw a beautiful building that looked like a castle.
I'll bet it's full of knights and kings!
But inside, it was no castle. It was packed full of people speaking all kinds of strange languages and wearing funny clothes.

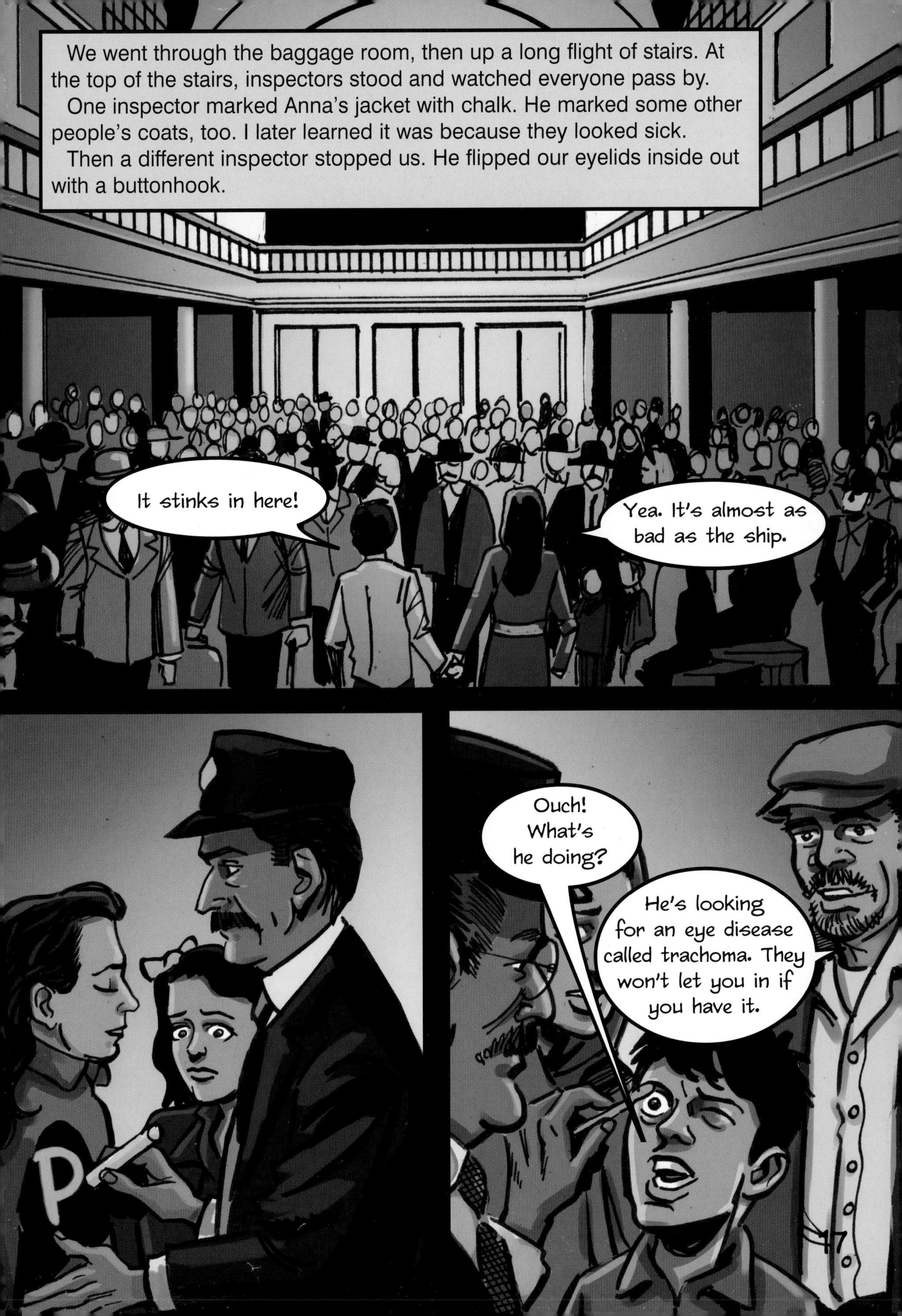
We went through the baggage room, then up a long flight of stairs. At the top of the stairs, inspectors stood and watched everyone pass by.
One inspector marked Anna's jacket with chalk. He marked some other people's coats, too. I later learned it was because they looked sick.
Then a different inspector stopped us. He flipped our eyelids inside out with a buttonhook.
It stinks in here!
Yea. It's almost as bad as the ship.
P
Ouch! What's he doing?
He's looking for an eye disease called trachoma. They won't let you in if you have it.

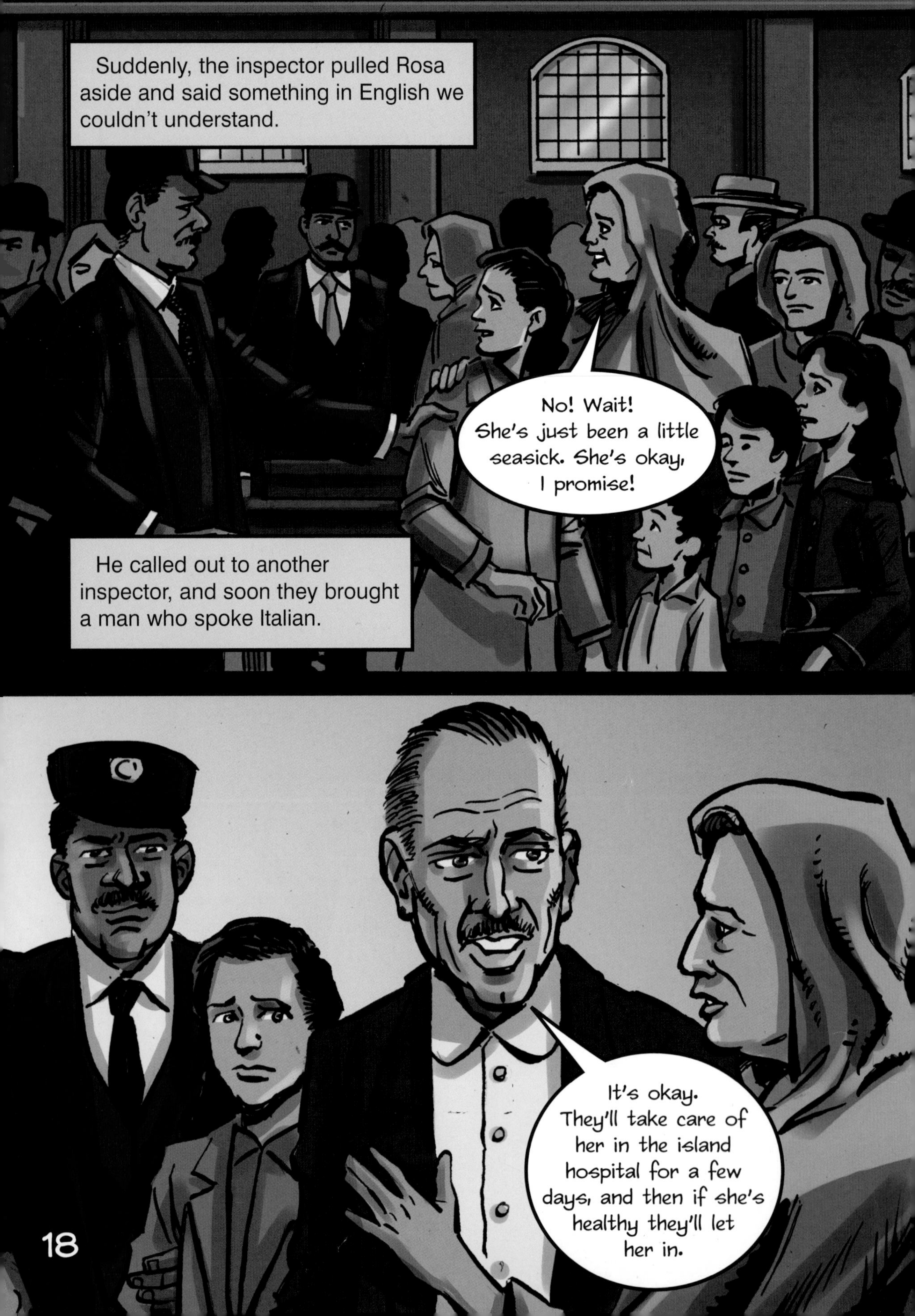
Suddenly, the inspector pulled Rosa aside and said something in English we couldn't understand.
No! Wait! She's just been a little seasick. She's okay, I promise!
He called out to another inspector, and soon they brought a man who spoke Italian.
It's okay. They'll take care of her in the island hospital for a few days, and then if she's healthy they'll let her in.

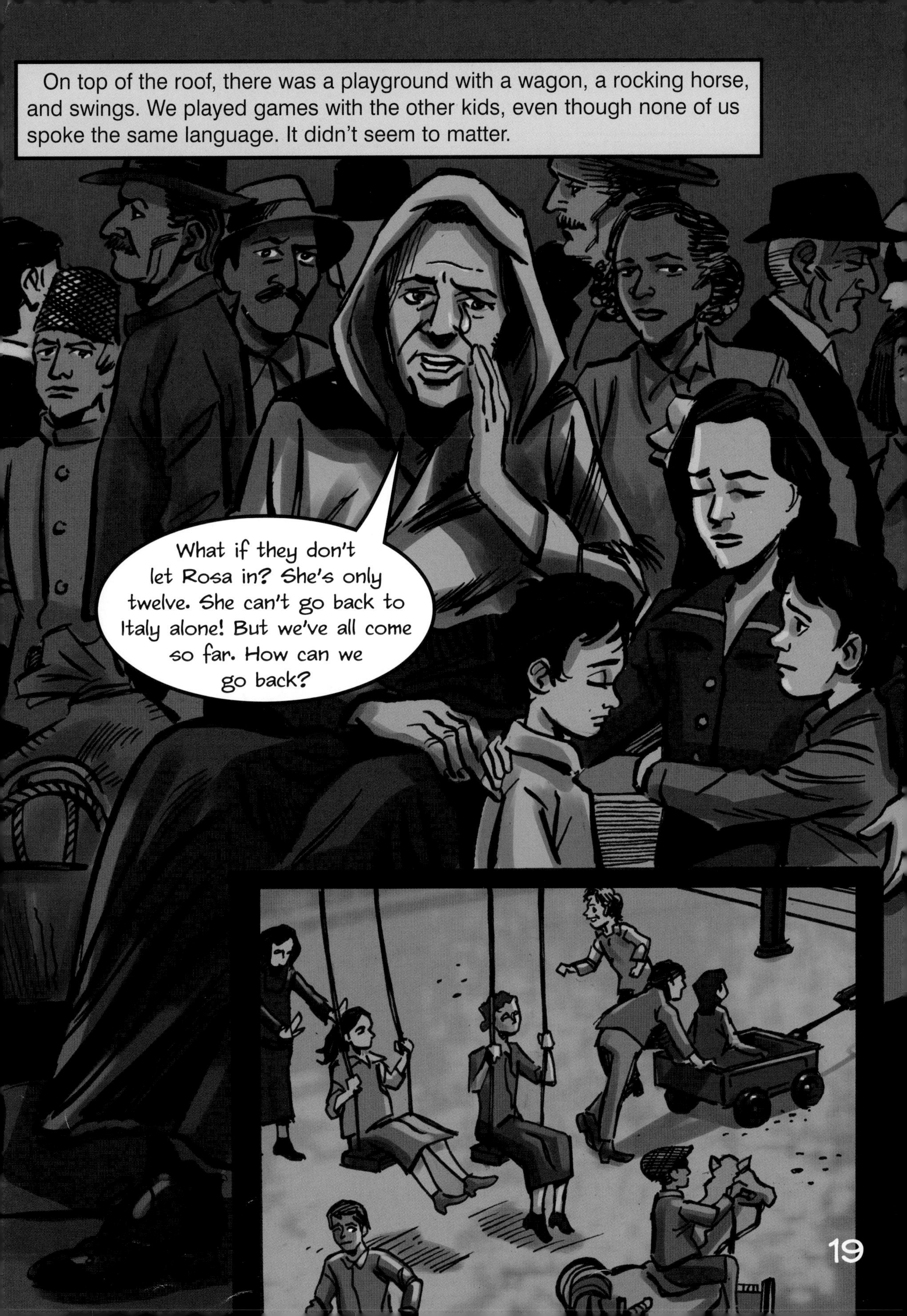
On top of the roof, there was a playground with a wagon, a rocking horse, and swings. We played games with the other kids, even though none of us spoke the same language. It didn't seem to matter.
What if they don't let Rosa in? She's only twelve. She can't go back to Italy alone! But we've all come so far. How can we go back?

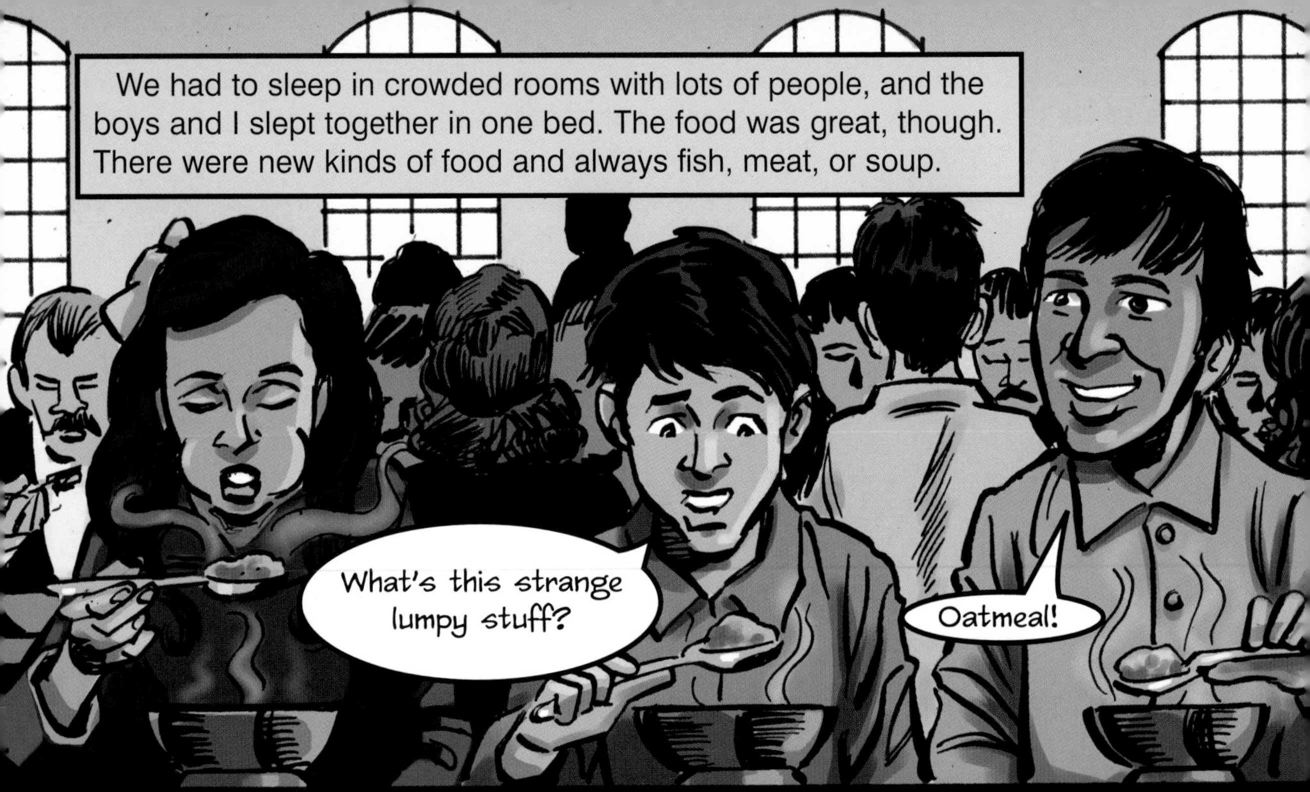
We had to sleep in crowded rooms with lots of people, and the boys and I slept together in one bed. The food was great, though. There were new kinds of food and always fish, meat, or soup.
What's this strange lumpy stuff?
Oatmeal!

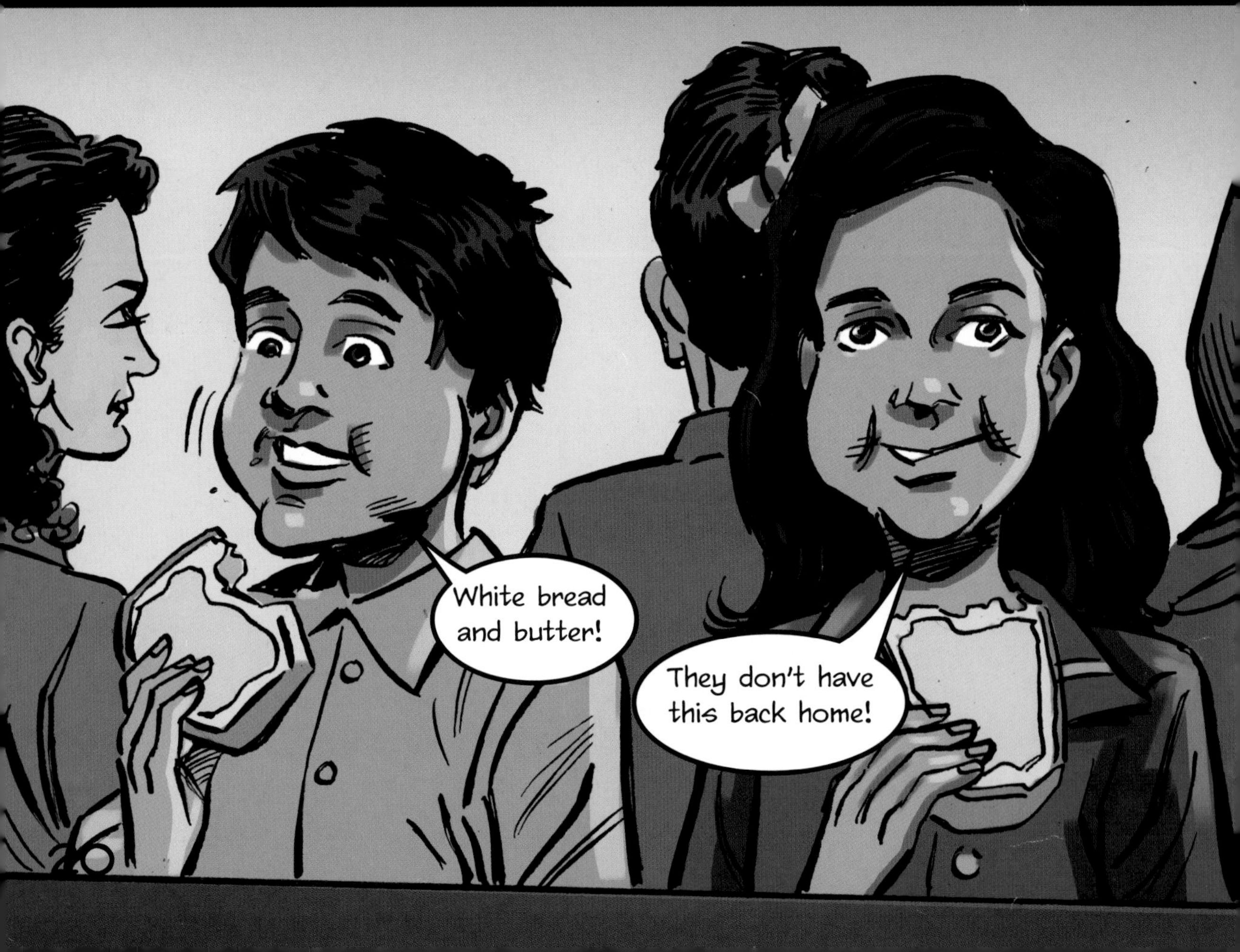
White bread and butter!
They don't have this back home!

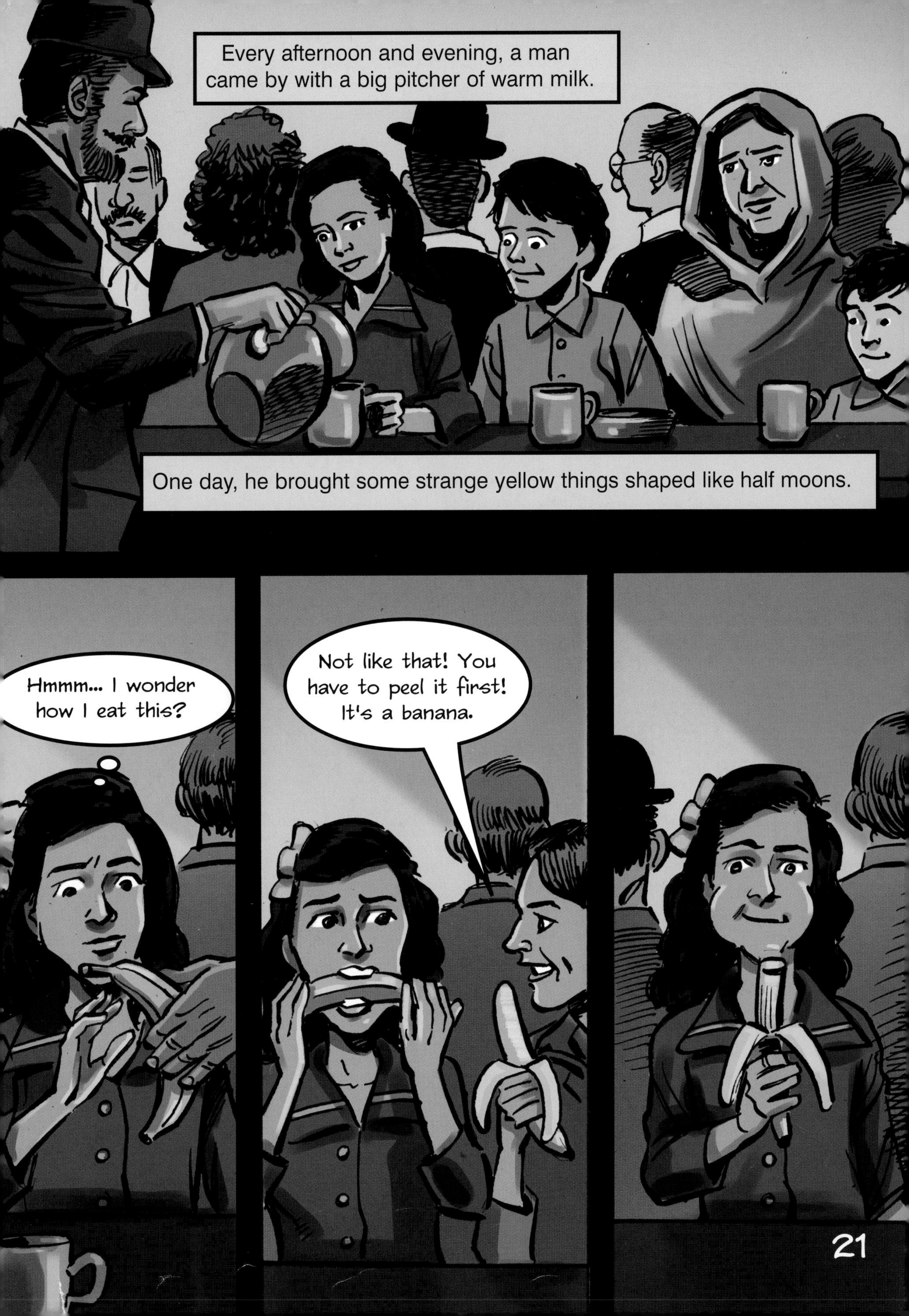
Every afternoon and evening, a man came by with a big pitcher of warm milk.
One day, he brought some strange yellow things shaped like half moons.
Hmmm... I wonder how I eat this?
Not like that! You have to peel it first! It's a banana.

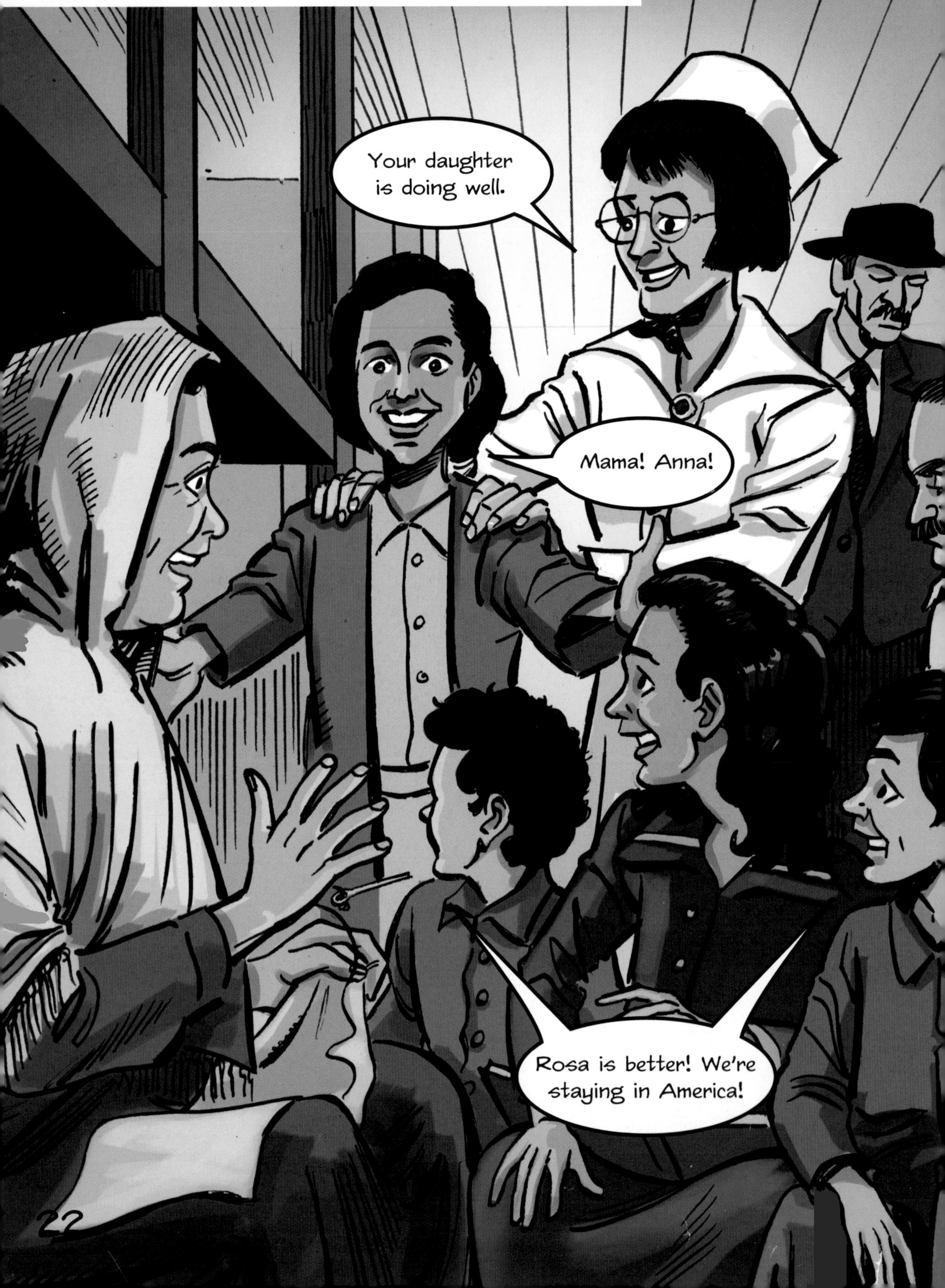
Your daughter is doing well.
Mama! Anna!
Rosa is better! We're staying in America!

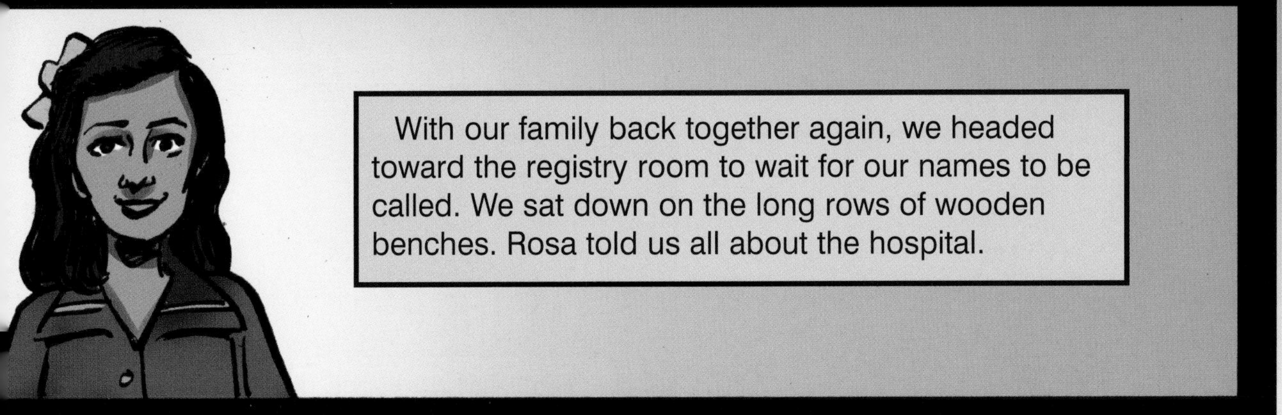
With our family back together again, we headed toward the registry room to wait for our names to be called. We sat down on the long rows of wooden benches. Rosa told us all about the hospital.

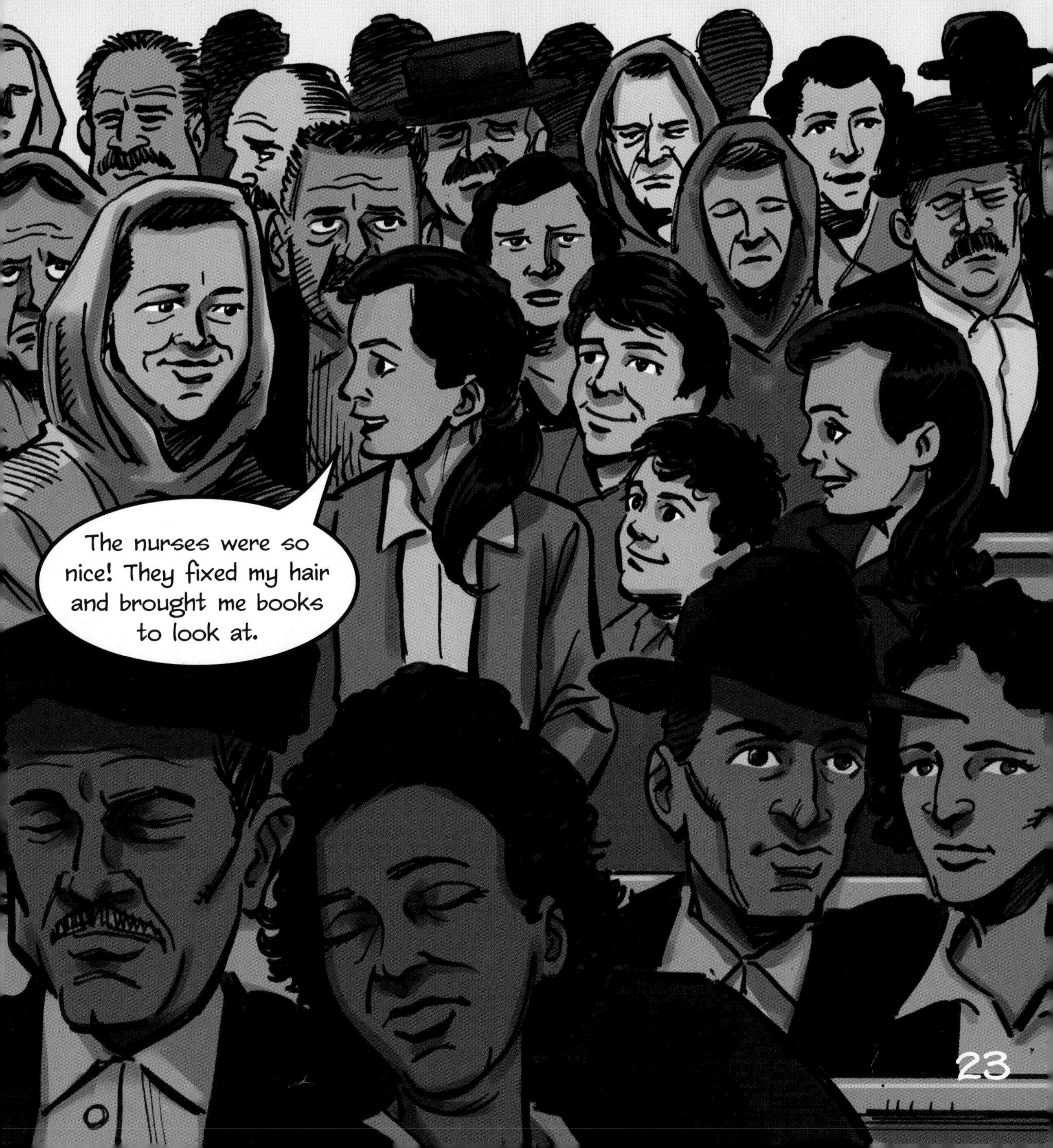
The nurses were so nice! They fixed my hair and brought me books to look at.

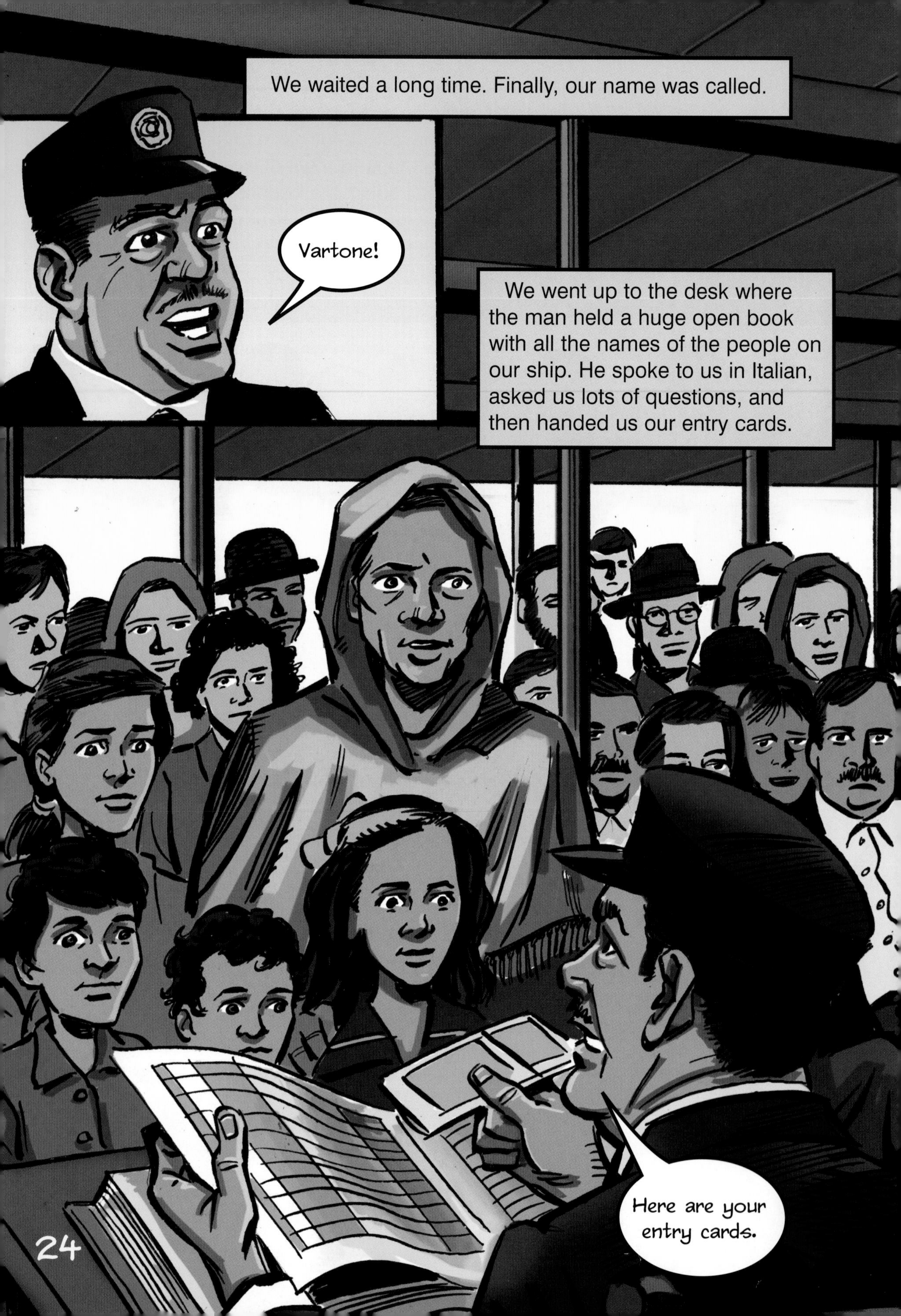
We waited a long time. Finally, our name was called.
Vartone!
We went up to the desk where the man held a huge open book with all the names of the people on our ship. He spoke to us in Italian, asked us lots of questions, and then handed us our entry cards.
Here are your entry cards.

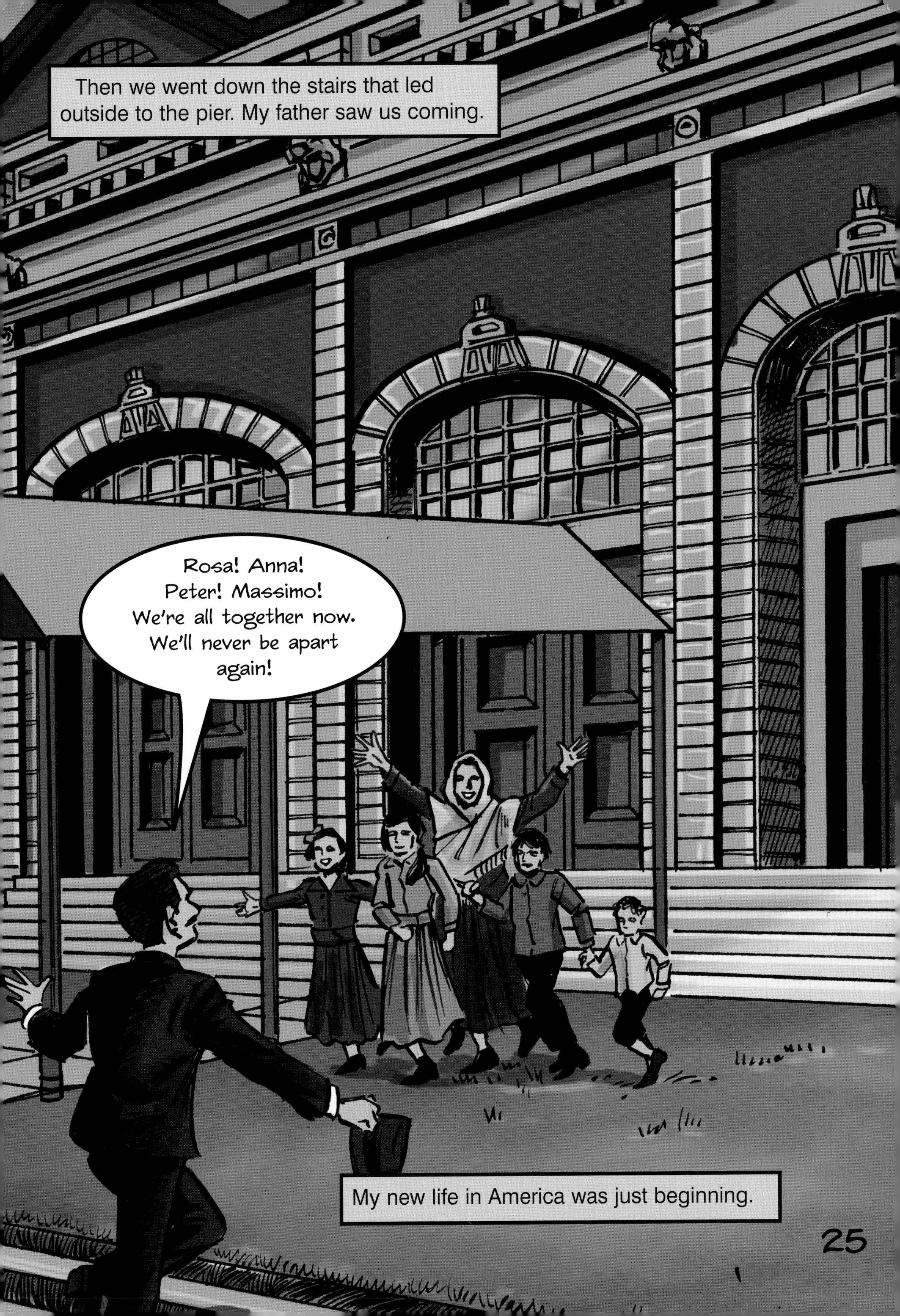

Then we went down the stairs that led outside to the pier. My father saw us coming.
Rosa! Anna! Peter! Massimo! We're all together now. We'll never be apart again!
My new life in America was just beginning.

Coming to America

During its peak year in 1907, more than one million immigrants passed through Ellis Island. They came from all over the world, speaking many languages and wearing traditional clothing from their homelands. As the number of immigrants entering increased, the island became crowded.

Immigrants waited in huge lines to receive permission to enter the United States.

Sometimes immigrants had to wait several days in port before ferries were able to take them to the island. However, most of the immigrants who arrived eventually made it through the island and into America.

In 1924, a new act called the National Origins Act required immigrants to go through medical exams and other inspections in their homeland before coming to the United States. They no longer needed to pass through immigration stations like Ellis Island. As a result, on November 12, 1954, Ellis Island was closed.

In 1965, Ellis Island became part of the Statue of Liberty National Monument. It is now a historical site that is governed by the United States National Park Service. It is located a half a mile north of Liberty Island, where the Statue of Liberty is located.

Present-day Ellis Island

Visitors to Ellis Island can tour inside the main building and see photographs and landing cards of the passengers. They can also tour the grounds and see the American Immigrant Wall of Honor. Over half a million names are inscribed on the wall of the immigrants who came through Ellis Island.

You can also see a bronze statue of 15-year-old Annie Moore, who was the first immigrant to enter America through Ellis Island. When she arrived on January 1, 1892, she was given a gold coin worth ten dollars. That was a lot of money in those days!

Buildings on Ellis Island

Ellis Island originally held a small military fort and was used to store **ammunition** during the Civil War. Workers cleared out the ammunition and brought in dirt and landfill to double the island's size.

The original wooden structure that they built burned down in 1897. Fortunately, no one was hurt, and new fireproof buildings were quickly put up.

Class Distinctions Among Immigrants

Onboard the ships headed to America, the poorer passengers had to ride in **steerage** class. The accommodations were often very dirty and unhealthy. Just a few dollars more could buy a ticket in second class, with clean, private rooms, but many immigrants couldn't afford the price.

When the ships arrived in New York harbor, the passengers in first and second class were taken immediately into New York City. They were not required to pass through Ellis Island like the poorer travelers.

Children from the steerage class played on the decks of ships.

Beware of the Chalk Marks

The marks that some people entering Ellis Island received on their clothing meant the difference between going back home or staying in America. The chart below shows what some of the marks meant.

X	for suspected mental illness	**H**	for heart
C	for conjunctivitis	**S**	for senility
Ct	for trachoma	**B**	for back
E	for eyes	**L**	for lameness
Ft	for feet	**Sc**	for scalp
		P	for physical and lungs

Websites

teacher.scholastic.com/activities/immigration/tour/stop1.htm

pbskids.org/bigapplehistory/immigration/topic7.html

www.nps.gov/elis/

www.ellisisland.org/

library.thinkquest.org/20619/Eihist.html

www.statueofliberty.org/Ellis_Museum.html

Glossary

ammunition (am-yuh-NISH-uhn): Bullets, gunpowder, cannons, bombs, and other explosive materials used in a war.

buttonhook (BUHT-unh-HUK): Small metal hooks used to pull buttons through the buttonholes on boots and gloves.

class (klass): A person's social standing or status in society, often related to how much money a person has.

ferry (FER-ee): A boat that carries people and objects across a short stretch of water. At Ellis Island, ferries carried passengers from the big steamships to the island shore.

immigrants (IM-uh-gruhnts): People who leave their native land in order to live in another country.

inspectors (in-SPEK-turz): People who examine or oversee something. The inspectors at Ellis Island examined the immigrants to make sure they were healthy and fit for life in the United States.

oppression (un-PRESH-uhn): The unfair or cruel use of power against another person or group of people.

poverty (POV-ur-tee): The state of being extremely poor.

steamship (STEEM-ship): A large boat driven by steam, or hot water vapor kept under pressure. Steamships were a very popular way to travel in the nineteenth and early twentieth centuries.

steerage (STIHR-uj): The bottom part of the steamship where the machinery for steering the boat is located.

Index

About the Author

Holly Karapetkova, Ph.D., loves writing books and poems for kids and adults. She teaches at Marymount University and lives in the Washington, D.C. area with her son K.J. and her two dogs, Muffy and Attila.

About the Illustrator

Pete McDonnell is an illustrator who has worked in his field for twenty-four years. He has been creating comics, storyboards, and pop-art style illustrations for clients such as Marvel Comics, the History Channel, Microsoft, Nestle, Sega, and many more. He lives in Sonoma County, California with his wife Shannon (also an illustrator) and son Jacob.